School R
from the
Black Lagoon

by Mike Thaler · pictures by Jared Lee

SCHOLASTIC INC.

New York   Toronto   London   Auckland   Sydney
Mexico City   New Delhi   Hong Kong   Buenos Aires

To Jeannie,

Knock, knock.

Who's there?

Olive.

Olive who?

Olive you!

—M.T.

To Larry and Hope Bone

—J.L.

ISBN-13: 0-978-0-545-01758-9
ISBN-10: 0-545-01758-0

Text copyright © 2007 by Mike Thaler.
Illustrations copyright © 2007 by Jared D. Lee Studio, Inc.

12 11 10 9 8 7 6 5 4 3 2 1   7 8 9 10 11 12/0

Printed in the U.S.A.
First printing, November 2007

Black Lagoon Elementary

Where do dolphins hang out at school?

The multiporpoise room

What's the worst animal to take a test with?

A cheetah

What do you call half a frog?

A frogtion

ASK ME A QUESTION.

MATH

What prehistoric animal could add, subtract, and multiply?

A mathadon

Why is an amoeba good at math?

It can divide.

If Hubie has 3 apple pies and he eats 2 of them, what does he have?

A stomachache

Why are rabbits good at math?

They multiply quickly.

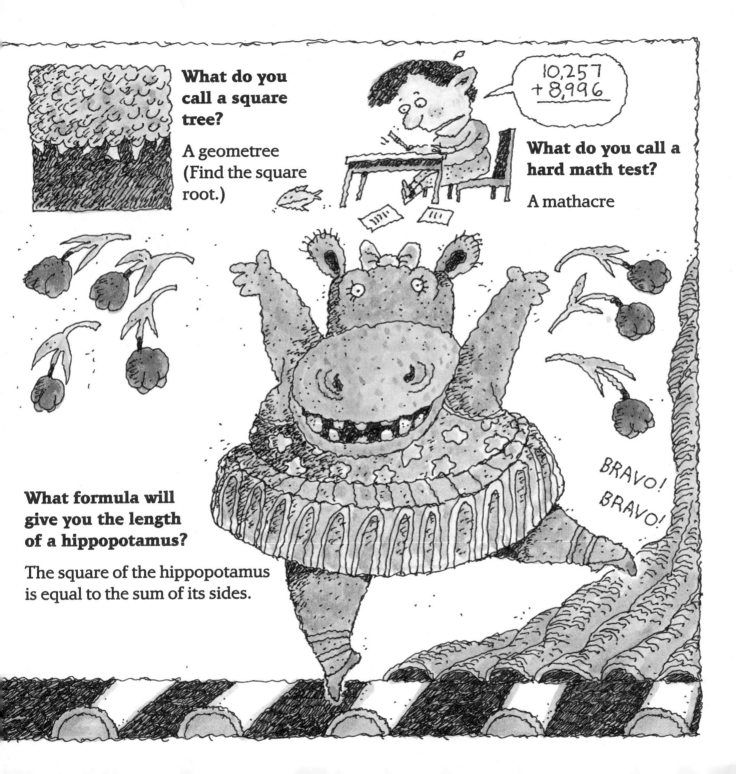

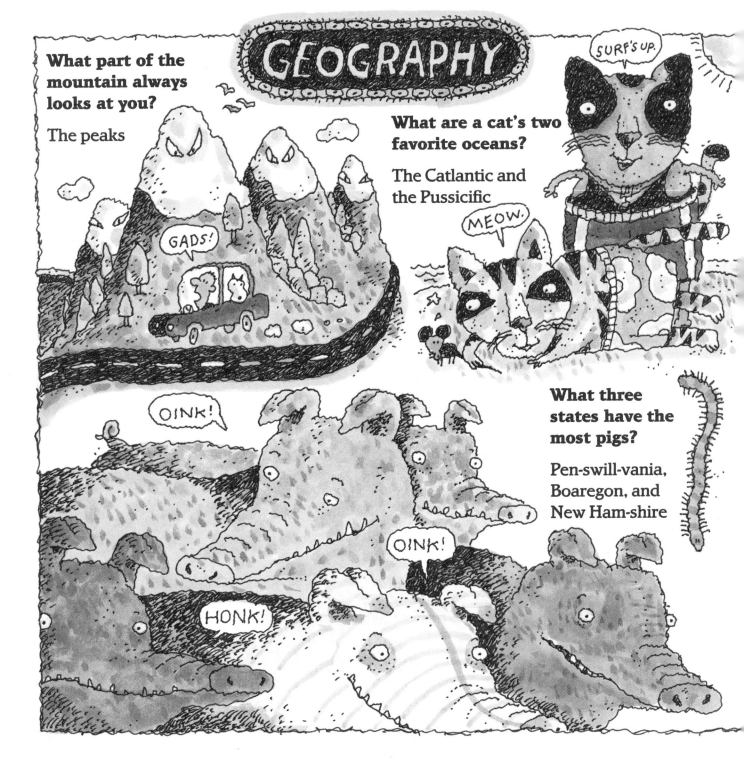

What three states have the most cows?

Cow-lifornia, Moosouri, and Cow-lorado

What state has the most married women?

Mrs.sippi

What city has the most dentists?

Toothon, Arizona

11

RECESS

What student is all over the schoolyard?

The class clone

Did Hubie have a good time at recess?

He had a ball.

What has 18 legs and catches flies?

A baseball team

OOPS!

What has ten legs and dribbles?

A basketball team

What has 12 legs and spikes?

A volleyball team

What's a giant ape's favorite game?

King Kong Ping Pong

15

What bone was a famous rock and roll star?

Pelvis

How do you stop a rhinoceros from charging?

Cancel his credit card.

What do you call spiders that just got married?

Newlywebs

Who is your coolest relative?

Aunt Arctica

COME FOR A VISIT.

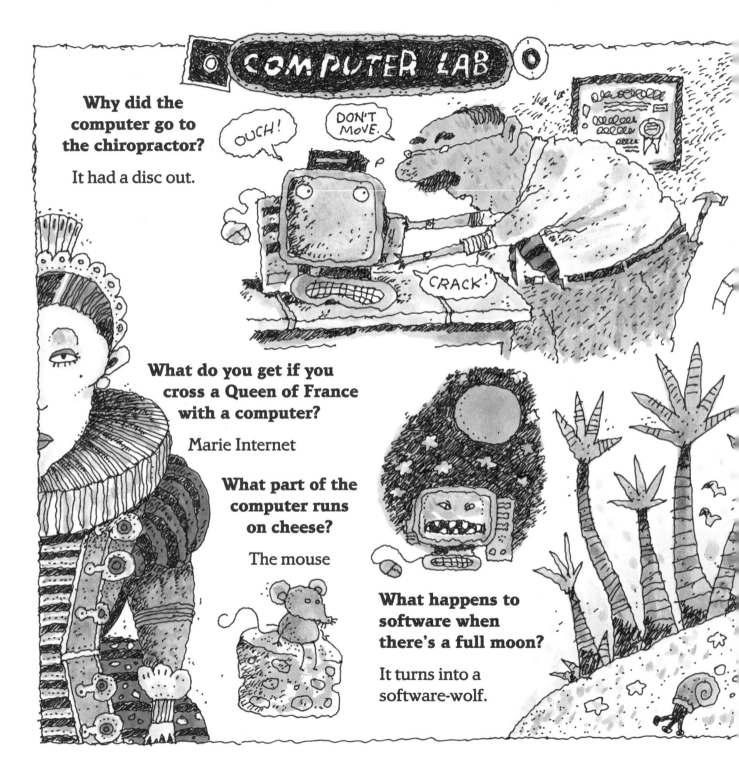

What did the Little Engine That Could say when it was learning to use the computer?

"I think icon. I think icon."

Why did Hubie wear a bathing suit to computer class?

To surf the Internet

Why are chapter books like dragons?

They have long tails.

Why is every book a champion?

Because they all have titles (Miss Universe, Heavyweight Champion, etc.)

Why did the monster eat the library?

Because he was hungry for knowledge.

Why was Hubie's nose sent to the principal's office?

For running in the hallways

Who belongs to the Black Lagoon P.T.A.?

Mummies and Deadies

What kind of car does Mrs. Green drive? A Lamborgoony

SNIFF SNIFF

WHAT DO YOU GET IF YOU CROSS...

A cow with a jumping bean?

A milk shake

A frog with a janitor?

A cus-toadian

A Roman Emperor with a head of lettuce?

A Caesar salad

An arctic bird with a writing instrument?

A ballpoint penguin

An alligator with a pickle?

A crocodill

← PICKLE

NOTEBOOK

An ocean with a kangaroo?

Wet!

A circus with a notebook?

A three-ring binder